SOCIAL STUDIES MATTERS!

WHAT IS CULTURE?

PETER FINN

PowerKiDS press

Published in 2024 by The Rosen Publishing Group, Inc.
2544 Clinton Street, Buffalo, NY 14224

First Edition

Editor: Therese Shea
Book Design: Michael Flynn

Photo Credits: Cover, p. 1 ooo.photography/Shutterstock.com; (series background) Eky Studio/Shutterstock.com; p. 5 Rawpixel.com/Shutterstock.com; p. 7 wayfarerlife/Shutterstock.com; p. 9 Sergey Novikov/Shutterstock.com; p. 11 Craig Sterken/Shutterstock.com; p. 13 Cat Us/Shutterstock.com; p. 15 Knot9Images/Shutterstock.com; p. 17 Werner Spremberg/Shutterstock.com; p. 19 Gorodenkoff/Shutterstock.com; p. 21 Anton Bielousov/Shutterstock.com.

Library of Congress Cataloging-in-Publication Data

Names: Finn, Peter, 1978- author.
Title: What is culture? / Peter Finn.
Description: New York : PowerKids Press, [2024] | Series: Social studies matters! | Includes index.
Identifiers: LCCN 2023031252 (print) | LCCN 2023031253 (ebook) | ISBN 9781499443868 (library binding) | ISBN 9781499443851 (paperback) | ISBN 9781499443875 (ebook)
Subjects: LCSH: Culture–Juvenile literature.
Classification: LCC GN357 .F532 2024 (print) | LCC GN357 (ebook) | DDC 306–dc23/eng/20230804
LC record available at https://lccn.loc.gov/2023031252
LC ebook record available at https://lccn.loc.gov/2023031253

Manufactured in the United States of America

CONTENTS

Ways of Life

Culture is all the ways of life of a group of people. Ways of life can include language, clothing, **traditions**, foods, music, arts, values, and beliefs. Your culture is all these things—and much, much more!

Where It Comes From

Culture is handed down from a past **generation**. Your parents are from the generation before you. They taught you certain ways of life. The generation before your parents passed down their ways of life. For example, some people wear clothing **styles** of past generations.

Languages

Language is a part of culture. It's how people **exchange** ideas. Language can mean speaking, writing, body movements, and sign languages. Some languages we learn as babies. Others we learn later. Languages can change over time. Words we use may come from other languages.

Ciao
Hello
Hello
Hola
Привет
Bonjour
Hallo

Traditions

Cultures can have **unique** traditions or traditions in common. Greek children throw their baby teeth on the roof for good luck. Many cultures in Asia, Eastern Europe, and the Middle East remove their shoes indoors. And many cultures around the world use fireworks for **celebrations**.

Foods

Cultures have special foods. Some foods are a part of cultures because of what grows around them. For example, rice is easy to grow in China. Corn grows well in Mexico. These foods are important to cultures in these places.

Beliefs and Values

Cultures have certain beliefs and values. Many people of a culture may follow a **religion**. This religion helps shape their beliefs about what's true. Values tell us what's important. Some cultures value family highly. Many generations of a family might live in one home.

Arts and Music

All cultures have arts and music. These can look and sound different. Sometimes this depends on where the culture is found. For example, **instruments** might be made from certain trees and animal skins. Some cultures have songs to teach, **entertain**, or heal the sick.

Cultures Change

Not everyone in a culture has the same ways of life. Cultures can change too. When people move, their culture can change. For example, they might dress or eat differently in their new home. Cultures also change when they come together. They exchange ideas.

Celebrate Culture!

Scientists called anthropologists study cultures. Some study past cultures. Others study cultures of today. You can learn about cultures too. Many cultures have celebrations that teach you about their ways of life. There's a lot to celebrate about world cultures!

SQUAMISH NATION
20
SQUAMISH NATION
3

GLOSSARY

celebration: A time to show happiness for an event through activities such as eating or playing music.

entertain: To do things that are interesting for people to watch or listen to.

exchange: To give something and get something in return.

generation: A group of individuals born about the same time.

instrument: An object used to make music.

religion: A belief in and way of honoring a god or gods.

style: A certain fashion or way of doing something.

tradition: A way of thinking or acting that's been used in a society for a long time.

unique: Special or different from anything else.

FOR MORE INFORMATION

BOOKS

Murray, Marie. *Culture and Diversity*. Minneapolis, MN: Free Spirit Publishing, 2020.

O'Brien, Cynthia. *Encyclopedia of American Indian History & Culture: Stories, Time Lines, Maps, and More*. Washington, D.C.: National Geographic, 2019.

Serres, Alain. *I Have the Right to Culture*. Berkeley, CA: House of Anansi Press, 2021.

WEBSITES

Culture Facts for Kids

kids.kiddle.co/Culture

Read more facts about the idea of culture.

Food Facts for Kids

www.kids-world-travel-guide.com/food-facts-for-kids.html

Explore cultures around the world through their foods.

INDEX